658.159
M813e

Lincoln Branch Library
1221 E. 7 Mile
Detroit, MI 48203

# Empowering You To Help

D1125085

LI

# Empowering You To Help

## Resources for Faith-Based Non-Profits
### Connecting You to Your Community

Jenai A. Morehead

iUniverse, Inc.
New York   Bloomington

**Empowering You To Help**
**Resources for Faith-Based Non-Profits**

Copyright © 2003, 2008 by Jenai Morehead

iUniverse books may be ordered through booksellers or by contacting:

iUniverse
1663 Liberty Drive
Bloomington, IN 47403
www.iuniverse.com
1-800-Authors (1-800-288-4677)

ISBN: 978-0-595-27687-5 (pbk)

Printed in the United States of America

# Contents

# How I Started Writing Grants

As a grant writer I receive numerous requests to write grants and consult on projects. The question I am often asked is, "How did you become a grant writer?" To say the least, the answer is quite humbling.

Our young church was in a building fund drive directed by a gifted fundraiser who was a member of our growing church All power was given to our fledgling member to make the connections necessary to raise funds. Unfortunately a disastrous relationship within our church caused her to put all fundraising projects on hold and our building fund project came to a screeching halt. Within days the potential for making thousands of dollars toward our project was gone.

Many days of anger ensued and I asked God to give me her gift so I could use it to regain our lost funds. I spent many days recounting the story in my mind and angrily complaining to God. He quietly listened to me. One day I realized that I was asking in vain.

I wanted God's power to spite someone and there was no glory in it for God. I repented and God gave me a wonderful gift with the condition that the relationship between Him and me had to be close in order for me to write. He would bless me with the ability to gain wealth and I would be subject to His judgment if I used my gift outside of His will. (Deuteronomy 8:18)

The first grant I wrote with Dr. Morehead was for $1.8 million dollars worth of property. We asked the Federal government for a church and gym facility that was being abandoned due to the Base Closure Act. The modern buildings were awarded to the church. The rest is history in the making.

# CHAPTER 1

# Before You Begin

I want you to understand that this book is a guide to changing your faith-based program from just a dream to a working community program.

There is a point at which you must stop planning and begin implementing your community programs, regardless of how much money or help you have. Your food program may begin with giving out bag lunches at the back door of your church and grow into a large food bank or feeding program. Whatever you do, you will need to start somewhere.

We began our community programs at our church. A couple of years later our church moved into a small office building. It had three small offices, a boardroom and a kitchen. One of the offices was dedicated to our community-based ventures. Our Deacon built a cabinet that was 4 by 12 feet. It held our baptismal clothing, food for the poor and our religious supplies. It was like the Ark of the Covenant. Wherever we moved it went with us. We had church outside in the courtyard in the mornings. In the evening we would jam into the halls and the boardroom with Pastor preaching in an open doorway. The boardroom was packed with people waiting to hear the Pastor. Behind him was a hallway lined with chairs to accommodate everyone who could not fit in the boardroom. When Pastor preached he would bounce backwards and forwards in the doorway so that everyone could see him. He used a karaoke machine for a sound system.

We purchased a phone and office supplies and asked two staff members to volunteer while the office was open from 8 a.m. to 5 p.m. We set August 12 as an opening date for our office and we were scared to death because our staff had never run an office all day long before. We had been content to just give out food, clothes and help homeless people intermittently. What else were we going to do?

On opening day we arrived, turned on the lights, chatted, shuffled some papers around and arranged our desks. After about an hour we began to look at each other.

Pastor said he would walk across the street to see what our city programs were. One co-worker said she needed something to do. I gave her our office phone book to re-write. I asked her to write slowly because there was nothing to do. When Pastor returned, he had forms and applications from the city and county economic development departments. We've never had a dull day since.

## Can My Church and Faith Based Organization Work Together?

I'll tackle this question right away since it is often burning on the minds of pastors and their administrators.

The good news is yes! The church and the non-profit can work together if certain guidelines can be followed.

Another question asked is: Do I have to start a community based or faith based non-profit to deliver services to my community or to get grant money?

The answer is no. Again, there are certain guidelines when it comes to the church getting grants for the delivery of services to the community. I will discuss the particulars later in chapter 5 (see: Working with Religious Organizations.)

# CHAPTER 2

# An Overview of the Private and Federal Grants Process

### *Helping Those in Need: An Overview of the Federal Grants Process*

If you are in the business of caring for people in need, you must understand that resources are necessary to do the work effectively. And chances are if you had a little more money, you would be able to help more people and do your work better. If you run an organization to help those in need, you may be eligible to receive Federal money through grant programs.

### *What kinds of grants are available from the Federal government?*

The Federal government uses two kinds of grants:

Grants handed out by an agency of the Federal government (also known as 'discretionary' grants)—for instance, a homeless assistance grant given out by the Department of Health and Human Services to a homeless shelter.

Grants that put federal money in the hands of states, cities, or counties for them to distribute to charities and other social service providers, usually under their own rules and regulations (also known as 'formula' or 'block' grants).

Therefore, you can apply directly to the Federal government or you can apply for funds to an entity that distributes money it receives from the Federal government.

### *How can my organization find out about Federal grants?*

The White House Office of Faith-Based and Community Initiatives has prepared a list of general information on about 100 programs operated by the Departments of Justice, Labor, Health and Human Services, Housing and Urban Development, and Education. You may access this information by visiting **www.fbci.gov**. It includes programs from these agencies that are of interest to small, grassroots groups. Use this list as a starting point to find out about opportunities that may interest you.

Once you find a program that interests you, you can get more information about when and how you can apply for funds from the agency contact in the listing. You can also use the *Catalog of Federal Domestic Assistance*, or CFDA, as a resource which also lists grants by agencies.

## How do I go about applying for a federal grant?

All federal grants must be announced to the public. These announcements (sometimes called a "Program Announcement," "Request for Proposal," "Notice of Funding Availability," or "Solicitation for Grant Applications") are the Federal government's way of looking for charities and other groups to provide a federally funded service.

Today, Grants.gov is a central storehouse for information on over 1,000 grant programs and provides access to approximately $400 billion in annual awards. Registering will take you through a process to prepare for applying for a federal grant. Each grant announcement will contain instructions on how to apply, including where to get an application packet, information the application should contain, the date the application is due, and the agency contact information.

The *Catalog of Federal Domestic Assistance* (**www.cfda.gov**) also contains information about grant announcements. In addition, agency web sites contain information on funding opportunities. In particular, faith-based and community groups should check for information on the web sites for the White House Office of Faith-Based and Community Initiatives (**www.fbci.gov**), as well as on the web sites for the agency centers.

Many states and cities also have liaisons that can help faith-based and community applicants identify grant opportunities.

## We are a small organization and we can't afford to hire a grant writer, accountant, and lawyer to help us seek a Federal grant. Is there any help for us?

Most federal agencies have experts who are available to help organizations apply for and manage their grants. Applicants may call the official identified in the grant announcement or contact an agency's regional office. The agency staff is available to answer questions over the phone. They may also refer applicants to local or nearby technical assistance workshops or to organizations that are under contract with the Federal government to provide this kind of assistance.

Assistance may also be available from one of the nearly two dozen organizations funded by the Department of Health and Human Services Compassion Capital Fund. These organizations help small faith-based and community organizations learn about the grants process. They may also help small groups with other challenges, such as training volunteers and staff or expanding the reach of the services they provide. They do this at no cost to your organization. You can learn more about the Compassion Capital Fund and the organizations it funds at **www.hhs.gov/fbci**.

In addition, for general questions about writing a grant proposal, many state governments and cities provide grant-writing workshops, as do a number of nonprofit organizations and foundations.

### *Is there any money specifically set aside for faith-based organizations?*

No. While there are small programs like the Compassion Capital Fund that are designed to help faith-based and community groups with the challenges they face, the Federal government does not set aside funds specifically for those groups. However, each year hundreds of millions of dollars go to religious charities and grassroots groups to provide vital federal services for the poor. The government does not ask, "Does your organization believe in God?" It asks, "Does your program work? Does it meet the specific requirements of the grant? Is it turning peoples' lives around? Is it accountable for the money it receives?"

There are three things every church should do to ensure adequate funding of external programs: 1) Self-fund. Ensure that you can adequately fund your program and that you come up with ways for your community programs to raise its own operating income. 2) Organize for additional help from banking institutions that lend to religious organizations. 3) Do not make grants your main source of income. Periodically you may have years that do not bring in as many grants. You will have to have a backup plan in place or a monetary reserve to meet your budget.

### *What if I apply for a Federal grant, but my request is turned down?*

There is no guarantee you will receive a grant if you apply. However, if you do not receive a grant, you should try to find out why you did not receive funding and how you could improve a future application. You can follow up with the program officer identified in the announcement. This individual will either be able to provide you with information about your application, or point you to the right person to contact. In addition, you may even be able to obtain written comments on your proposal, which could be a good learning tool.

Remember that many, many organizations compete for federal funds, and many groups apply several times before they receive an award. Getting feedback on your application can help you improve your chances of receiving funds the next time around.

### What are some of the legal obligations that come along with a Federal grant?

*Financial Reporting Requirements.* To make sure that grant funds are used properly, organizations that receive federal funds must file regular financial status reports. These forms should not take long to fill out, but they are important. The basic financial report form is a one-page document called *"Standard Form 269"*. Many agencies have adapted this form to suit their own programs. You can find a copy of "Standard Form 269" at **www. whitehouse.gov/omb/grants/#forms**.

*Audit.* All faith-based and community groups that receive federal funds are subject to basic audit requirements. These audits are intended to examine the federally funded parts of an organization's operations. The audits are necessary to make sure that federal dollars have been spent properly on legitimate costs. It is therefore extremely important for grant recipients to keep accurate records of all transactions conducted with federal funds.

The government itself does not audit most organizations, although the Federal government has the right to audit any program that receives public money at any time. For example, charities that spend less than $500,000 a year in federal funds are generally asked only to perform a "self-audit." For larger grants — those over $500,000 a year — an audit by a private, independent legal or accounting firm is required.

(Source: White House Office of Faith Based Initiatives: "Guidance To Faith Based and Community Organizations on Partnering with the Federal government")

## A word about "Free" government money for business or individuals

I cannot tell you the amount of times I have been asked about free money for business. Please do not fall for the scam. I have taken the time to give you a few excerpts from an internet article by Karen E. Klein of Business Week

### The Myth of Free Government Money: A Perennial and Pernicious Scam

"Seminar sellers and book hucksters routinely con people into shelling out hundreds of dollars to hear lectures or purchase directories that contain information readily available (yes, really for free!) in any public library or on the Internet."

"Common sense and the most basic awareness of business principles should tell entrepreneurs that no one besides Mom and Dad (maybe) will give you no-strings money to start a for-profit business. "If the government was in the position of providing all of the funds for free to people who start their own businesses, we wouldn't last long," says Mike Stamler, a spokesman for the U.S. Small Business Administration in Washington, D.C. "Not to mention that the American people would never stand for the government setting individuals up in business at no cost, and all at taxpayer risk."

"Still, the free-money hucksters find ready victims because people want to believe there's a way around the hard work of raising capital."So many people say they heard it from a friend or saw it on TV. Of course, they've never actually met anyone who got any free money. It becomes like the Holy Grail of small business, and a lot of entrepreneurs get caught up in this idea that it's out there," Rooney says. Rooney says he once ordered a "free-money" book advertised on television. The author claimed every entrepreneur was entitled to a government grant. Rooney received a directory of farmer's subsidies, Housing & Urban Development programs, and government-loan applications."

For more information on funding for startups, visit the SBA's Web site at www.sba.gov. It features extensive information on small-business loans and startup funding. For information on venture capital, visit the Venture Capital Resource Library, www.vfinance.com, the Capital Network, www.thecapitalnetwork.com, or Garage.com, www.garage.com.

### Private Grants Overview

Private grants are mainly given from foundations and corporations. A foundation is an entity that is established as a nonprofit corporation or a charitable trust, with a principal purpose of making grants to unrelated organizations or institutions or to individuals for scientific, educational, cultural, religious, or other charitable purposes. This definition encompasses two foundation types: private foundations and public foundations. The most common distinguishing characteristic of a private foundation is that most of its funds come from one source, whether an individual, a family, or a corporation. A public foundation, in contrast, normally receives its assets from multiple sources, which may include private foundations, individuals, government agencies, and fees for service. Moreover, a public foundation must continue to seek money from diverse sources in order to retain its public status.

There are many databases for private foundation; Foundation Center (foundationcenter.org) is one of the largest databases and points of information for foundations and grants training.

Whether you write a federal grant or a private one the same guidelines apply as to following directions and applying the professional rules of grant writing

Faith-based programs are not new. They are thousands of years old. A long time ago people of faith decided that they would serve their communities with the convictions that lied within their hearts regardless of the resources that were at hand.

Faith-based programs are programs based on the "substance of things hoped for, the evidence of things not seen". Faith is the medium by which we obtain what we need from God. It is the spiritual money that we give Him in exchange for the things that we hope for.

The Bible tells us that if we have pity on the poor, you lend to the Lord (Proverbs 19:17). God always repays his loans with more interest than you can ever dream of. Throughout the Bible, God expects us to help people who are less fortunate than we are. The poor extend far past the four walls of our congregations. They have particular needs that span across culture and time and the communities they occupy. Only people like you can understand their needs because you see them every day.

In our case we hoped for a homeless program, but could not see it. We believed that God would give us what we hoped for and we planned for it. Substance was given to our hope in the form of funding for our community programs.

It's no secret that the faith based community has been doing the lion's share of community work without the recognition or the money that many secular organizations have. It is our faith in challenging times which has helped our communities pull together when things didn't seem to make sense in our own backyards. It is because of your faith that people come to your door to get help.

Our local newspaper was interviewing us and they asked what obstacles we foresaw being a faith-based organization. I shared with them that although our grantors prohibited us from proselytizing, our clients saw the lives we lived and undoubtedly asked us about our faith. I explained that I have never seen an atheist in a foxhole. Rough times change and humble people; love softens the heart and covers a multitude of sin.

Just as I have never seen an atheist in a foxhole; I have never seen a grantor or government entity prohibit love, joy, peace, longsuffering, gentleness, goodness, faith, meekness and temperance: there is no law against these (Galatians 5:22).

# CHAPTER 3

# Before You Begin Writing

Before you begin writing anything, meet with your staff, volunteers or board to find out what community ideas and programs they are interested in doing. Examine your motives and ask yourself why you want to run a community based or faith-based organization.

Do you want to raise money?
Do you want to increase your membership?
Do you want to serve people and fill a need?
Do you want to be obedient to the word of God in taking care of the poor?

I read an article by Rev. E.V. Hill many years ago. He set the tone for what to expect from people that you are helping. He cautioned churches that are doing community work, not to expect the people they help to become members of your churches. Your church will not be built on your programs. Your membership will not increase because you have a soup kitchen or a housing program. Your church will be built on the word of God and the same outreach that exploded the church in the Book of Acts.

In your ventures approach everything **with hard work and faith.** You will be surprised what God can do. Be prepared to work past impossible odds and people telling you No! and absolutely not! Listen to God, he will tell you YES! You have his heart because you are helping poor and disadvantaged people who he loves.

In the beginning you will need to start with deciding a few things that are necessary to begin your non-profit. When in doubt seek professional advice from a qualified attorney, CPA or consultant.

1.  Choose a name for your organization. Please be very careful in choosing an appropriate name. Use wisdom. You want grantors to be comfortable with it and you want people to associate the name of your faith-based organization with community efforts.

2. Choose a board of directors: Make sure you have a good board of people with some experience in the services you are providing. After choosing your board, have your first board meeting.
3. Draft Articles and Bylaws for your organization.
4. File for your 501 (3) (c) tax exemption.
5. Create an intake system in order to collect information on the people you help. This information is the lifeblood of your organization. Without it you will not be able to show that you assist people.
6. Make sure you have the basic technology and office machines to enable you and your staff to access the internet and adequately communicate to others in a professional and timely manner. This is very important since time is money and knowledge is power. The proper use of technology will save you time and increase the possibility of you obtaining money.

## Matching Your Passion with Your Funding Source

In discussions with church leaders and staff across the country, I found that there were many passions and ideas. I presented a question to them. Do those passions fit into the framework of 1) the vision of your leaders, 2) the framework of the community, and 3) your organization's experience and professional background?

## Vision

Visionaries are important

If you are inspired to begin a community program ask your director/pastor what is the direction or vision he/she has for the community. What type of things would your visionary like to see in the community he/she is ministering in? The visionary is the beginning of your program. They are the catalyst that God will use to cause things to flow.

I admonish you to respect the vision and the visionary God has given you to work with (Jeremiah 3:15).

Remember no matter how talented you are, without a vision the people perish (Proverbs 29:18).

## The Framework of Your Community

Every city or town in the world is different. There are different demographics to each place in the world. Find out about the place you live in. What is the ethnicity? How many people are in the area you live in. How is the area divided geographically? Who are your community leaders and what area do they govern over? Answering these questions is important in helping you understand how to assist the people in your community.

Every community has a plan of action for growth

Every community has a plan for its growth and development. That plan is found in your city or town's economic development offices. This is the branch most likely to be concerned with carrying out the wishes of your city's leadership when it comes to growth and development. This is also the branch of your city that will work with government agencies that give your city money to develop economic and community plans. With these economic plans your city can work with non-profits to develop plans to assist low-income people.

Every few years your economic department must report to the Federal government on what the economic plan is for the area. This plan is usually for the next three to five years and often published and kept in the library and are available for public viewing.

It is very important to review this document because it often lists the priorities of your city fathers. Here you will find at least three to five priorities that will include employment for the citizens of the community, increased housing opportunities, the elimination of blight, public safety and the repair of streets and sewers.

This document is the collective direction your city would like to go in. It also tells the Federal government what your city will be spending federal dollars on.

Reading this document will give you a heads up on how to work effectively with your government in assisting the needs of people in your community. Knowing the priorities of your community leaders may also steer your organizational goals. If your city has any grant programs for community organizations, you can be assured that they will be looking for organizations that have the same priorities that they do.

If you know your city has a gang problem and gang intervention is the priority, and you have experience and the professional background for this job, you may want to direct your efforts toward that goal. If your goals do not match up with your community's then you might include some of your city's priorities as a set of sub-goals. If gang intervention is your organizations priority and getting rid of blight is a priority with your city you may be able to combine the two in outreach efforts to guide gang members to help clean up graffiti or trash in neighborhoods. Including your city's priorities in your grant narrative is very important. It lets the reader know that you are interested in your community as a whole and are willing to work together with city leaders to get the job done.

Grants are now asking very specific information about your community and the priorities in your towns and cities. You must be able to answer these questions intelligently using materials that will give you accurate information. Your grantor often has this information at their fingertips and can easily verify how much you know about the area you serve.

## Your Organization's Experience and Professional Background

Surround yourself with people of faith and purpose

Surrounding yourself with people of faith and purpose is important. One year I asked the Lord for $190,000 for several community projects by December. The loss of these projects would cause several families to be homeless and a drastic reduction in the services we provided to our community. I specifically asked God to give our organization funds and give our clients money and credit to purchase the homes we were leasing for them. Our clients began to pray with members of our board and staff vigilantly. Prayer meetings started breaking out all over the place. People began fasting and believing that God could perform a miracle. By October there was still no money and I was constantly before the Lord with our request. By December I received two letters granting our organization $191,000! One by one our formerly homeless clients began receiving loan approvals for mortgage loans to purchase their housing.

Whether you are a novice or an expert at what you do make sure that your board and staff have related experience in the projects that your organization is pursuing. Besides experience, wisdom is the important thing that your board should be able to supply. Naysayers and the pessimistic need not apply. Board members should be willing to volunteer their time for the cause they support. In the beginning your board may not look like that. They may not have the professional background you desire, but it will come as your organization grows.

Some churches or organizations surround themselves with board members that are the same faith. There is nothing wrong with this. Because you are faith-based many people on boards feel comfortable with people who have the same faith-level or who think alike as far as their religious beliefs. The Civil Rights Act gives religious groups protection in hiring people of the same faith to work in religious establishments. While you can hire people of the same faith take care not to discriminate against your brethren because of race or gender. There is no spiritual or federal protection for unlawful discrimination.

The important thing to remember is that you must have sound, professional people around you who are believers that God can do anything and that nothing is impossible. They must believe that they can do all things through Christ, which strengthens them. When the situation looks impossible, you need people who will pray and work to get through each day. Look at the people Jesus had around him. He had doctors, tax people and self-employed professionals. His disciples were business people who knew the lingo to communicate professionally with other business people.

Our professional background was in housing. We invested wisely in low-income areas and learned how to repair dilapidated housing. We learned how to subcontract and do much of the work ourselves. In doing so we rented to low-income families.

We learned how to work with people who were in poverty and understand the circumstances of how they arrived in it.

Your professional background might be in counseling, job development or youth programs. All of your staff and board's experience (paid or volunteer) translates into organizational experience. Be sure to document this by collecting resumes on all of your staff and board members.

Other things to consider:

a.  Are there prerequisites for applying for the funding source you are interested in?
b.  Are you the type of organization your grantor would like to fund?
c.  Are you asking for something that your grantor can offer?
d.  Do you understand the limitations and responsibilities of your grantor? (Geographic or monetary)
e.  Do your interests and your grantor's match?
f.  Can you be fiscally responsible with the money you are asking for?

Answering these questions is very important to begin the thinking process for your plans. Even if you do not have all the answers, being prepared will point you in the right direction.

# CHAPTER 4

# Grant Writing Suggestions

I have been a professional grant writer for many years and I have found that the best grant writer for your organization is YOU. There are three stages to grant writing:

1. Research: This is where you search for the right funding program for your organization. This also requires touching bases, meeting or calling with funders to explore their requirements in detail. This is the most time consuming part of grant writing and causes many organizations to drop out because they do not have the staff or the money to pursue more opportunities.
2. Grant Writing: The best writers are your team. You know your history and all the particulars about your program. Here is where you and your team can use your heads together to make a successful application. If you believe in yourself and apply good English skills toward your proposal you can be successful.
3. Compilation and review: This is the final review of all your work. It includes putting together the application and other papers requested by your grantor and a final look-over before turning in your application.

Grant development is a highly competitive field because many organizations are competing for the same funds. Only the best will win. Here are some tips to gain an edge for your proposal.

The fastest and easiest way to lean how to write a grant is to attend the training conference covering the specific grant you are interested in. The organization giving you money is the best source for information on how to ask for it.

Grant writing conferences help you with the two most important parts of your grant; the narrative and the budget. They help you to write good proposals that make sense and budgets that match the information in the narrative.

## Proposals must be realistic

What most grant writers do not realize is that there is a great difference between the writing of a proposal and the implementation of the program. After your grant is accepted another process begins. That process is almost as arduous as the writing process. That's the process in which you must prove everything you said. If your submissions are not acceptable with your grantor and realistic, then your grant request can be denied or lowered.

## What is your grantor looking for in the proposal?

1. The length and experience of your organization and/or the sponsors and partners of your project. This is called organizational capacity.
2. Goals and objectives for your intended project.
3. A narrative of your program. This is what I call the song and dance. This is one of the places where you get to really explain your program.
4. A budget. Your budget should be reasonable and it should make sense. You should provide a short narrative on your budget and explain it in simple terms.

Please be sure you critique your proposal before you send it to your grantors. Make several copies and have people read them. I guarantee they will be able to help you with grammar, errors and making common sense. A common error is not providing the grantor with the information they asked for. When an application asks you a question; please answer it directly. For example: I reviewed an application that simply asked for the area the non-profit served. The nonprofit went into a long dissertation on the geographic details of the area where the nonprofit was physically located. All the grantor wanted was the name of the area(s) they served. They did not answer the question and lost points.

## Searching for Mr. Right

Searching for the right grant is like looking for Mr. Right. He's out there.

In searching for grant opportunities make sure you meet the specifications of the grant. Organizations often make the mistake of trying to conform to a grant that they do not have the background for. Speak to the grant originators to find out about the grant itself. See if they like your ideas. Share with them why you believe you can do this project. In my years of grant writing I have only been awarded one grant that I did not personally have contact with the staff of the grantor. Human contact is paramount. When I see an agency I see people I can touch and move. It is people who will read your proposal. You must move them into believing that you can do the job.

I hope it has become obvious that the important thing to do is to plan and research. Planning and research is going to maximize your efforts to have a successful proposal and community program.

Your faith is important here in several ways. Up to this point you have trusted God for the formation of your faith based organization. Now you have to use the skills and wisdom that God gave you. You must also count on the instruction and advice you have obtained from good teachers.

By now you have been waiting for instructions on the perfect proposal. The form a grant takes on will be different every time. It will depend on the format your grantor chooses and the information they require. The grant proposal is a written account of the planning process for your program. Years ago, the old school method was to write your program. If you did not have much experience you may be able to get by with formulating your program on the way. Not true today! Today's grant requests ask tough questions that separate the novice from the expert. Narrative guidelines prompt the writer to have a program that is either already running or thoroughly planned out and ready to be implemented.

## Definition of a successful grant writer:

My teacher, Mr. Mike Dubose, of Research Associates said, "The most successful grant writers have built an impressive array of neurotic, obsessive, compulsive tendencies. They are organized (perfectionists) and seek other organized individuals to assist in projects. Grant writers have diversified backgrounds and build grant writing teams and agency processes. They will involve many different community volunteers, agency professionals and consumers in planning and program implementation. Grant writers are very receptive to new ideas. Most of all they have "Winning" as their middle name and they really love making money." I concur with all the above!

According to Dubose there are six things that will make your proposal successful:

• Creative ideas to prevent or reduce a community problem.

- Always help a targeted population and/or community.
- Attack problems through innovative and creative programs and services.
- Always seeking to expand a program and add a new twist for funding.
- Always learning new knowledge about how to prevent and reduce a problem.
- Sharing new knowledge to other key players, who in turn will benefit and impact other consumers and communities.

## When you write your proposal:

- **Read the instructions and follow the directions.** Read the instructions to the grant proposal very carefully and follow them strictly. If a proposal says type the grant in 12 pt. font, black ink, 1.5 double spacing, margins no more than 1 inch on all borders on recycled paper, then you must do it. Any deviation will get your proposal thrown out. There are professional reasons for every format. Following them will make life easier for the reader.
- **Make sure your reader understands your narrative:** Make sure your narrative is believable and realistic. Please type it. Write proposals clearly and to the point without lengthy and repetitive discussions.
- **Use Good Grammar and Get To The point:** When writing your proposal make sure the spelling and grammar is correct. Do not use meaningless or repetitive statements and big words unnecessarily. Do not try to impress your reviewers with too much data. Just present the data asked for to show that your proposal is solid and can be achieved.
- **Graphs, Figures, Calculations and Tables** Provide clear figures, calculations, and tables. Make sure they relate to your narrative.
- **Your budget** must reflect what is in your narrative.
- **Make sure** authorized personnel sign all the applicable certifications and documents. Include all the required documentation.
- **Make sure** all your paperwork is in order. Include a table of contents, index and tabs. Readers appreciate this.
- **Research**. Research is important in order to find your funds. The best place to start is your city or county economic development agency; grant research books at the library and on the Internet. Books written about your topic is a good place to get information.

## Pulling Your Reader In With A Good Narrative

When writing your narrative, pull the reader in emotionally about the need for a program such as yours in the community. Be passionate about what you do. Tell a short story about you or your board's experiences in homelessness, being without food, without clothing or legal help (whatever story applies to you).

Let other people who are not familiar with the project review your work. If they do not understand it or it is vague then chances are those who review your proposal will not understand it either. Many times the people who review your grant do not know you or your good intentions. Many times the people reviewing your proposal are citizen review committees that are not experts in writing proposals and program designs. If you have a chance to make corrections to your grant, based on the questions or concerns of your reviewers, your proposal will be a better one.

Do not refer to your program as an extension of a religious ministry of your church. While I stressed that your faith is important, your grantor does not want you to preach on their dime. It is all right to let your reader know the history of your organization if it was born out of your church or religious organization, just as ours was.

For specific parts of your program discuss alternative strategies and ideas to test your hypothesis. Try to spell out the shortcomings and problems in your proposal and how to solve them. Your readers will obviously see flaws in your grant and they will not be able to ask you questions since you may not be there while they read it. It is wise to anticipate their questions. If they see major challenges in your proposal, and there is no explanation on how to solve them, then your proposal will not be recommended for funding.

Be familiar with the demographics in your area. Know your population statistics. Know the statistics related to the people who you are serving. For example, know the number of females and males within each group and their ethnicity. How old are they? Are they single or do they have children? What are the chil-dren's ages? You will have to prove that you know about the demographics in your area. If you serve a specific population you will be required to know it in detail. If you serve parolees, for example, you must know about them as it pertains to your local area.

Government grants are different from private foundation grants. Foundations often require less writing and you may have a chance to explain to your reader's things they do not understand or correct mistakes you have made. Government grants require more writing and are often intense. Often you have one chance with government grants. The narratives and budgets are often detailed. Both are great sources of funding and I suggest taking advantage of both options.

If the grant is not funded contact the program director to find out why and if you can re-submit at a later date. This is a blessing in disguise. Any time you have the reason why your grant was not funded you will not make the same mistakes twice. Your chances of being funded the next time have increased greatly. Always get the rating of your grant and study to strengthen the weak part of your grant.

If the grant is funded, take your staff to lunch and thank them. Tell them what a good job they have done. Then tear apart the grant and beginthe business of running your program.

Here are a few reasons we do not obtain the grants we seek after.

- **Negative Attitude:** Your attitude determines how successful your proposal will be. A negative attitude will sabotage your proposal.
- **We are unaware of grant opportunities**: You must do research and stay informed.
- **Limited grant writing experience**: Get training and take courses.
- **There is no organized grant process**: Training will teach you how to organize.
- **Use of inadequate and outdated resources**: Always get the latest information via the Internet, newsletters or other published materials.
- **Inattention to details or instructions:** Pay attention to all the details.
- **Grant proposals that have not been edited or corrected in its final phase**: Have someone read your finished work to help you edit it.

## Grant Funding Resources

I must stress that Internet access is very important to the speed in which you do your research. It will allow you to access the volumes of information you will need to write your grants. I have spent hours and hours (the old fashioned way) researching information at my local library; pouring through volumes of books and magazines for valuable information. While there is no substitute for the library, I now appreciate the technology of the Internet that saves me time and money.

# CHAPTER 5

# Developing Your Dreams into Realistic Community Programs

When we began our ministry we knew it would be necessary to expand the vision into other areas of community work. Our staff became restless with just having church. They wanted to do more outreach and be able to provide direct help to the people in our community. Our visionary and pastor patiently listened and entertained all of our ideas and focused on the ones that would be best for our ministry to undertake. We decided that helping the homeless and low income families through housing and supportive services would be the best outreach for our community and faith-based organization. From there our non-profit was born.

We were real estate investors before being called to the ministry and we both had good jobs. The Lord blessed us with several pieces of rental property prior to being called to the pastorate. The demands of being a landlord, being employed full-time and working in the ministry began to wear thin on us. We needed help with our rental property. We decided to donate our real property to the church.

This move gave our church rental property and the organizational experience needed for future HUD contracts, in addition to raising the church's assets. Now the financial responsibility for the properties belonged to the church. Any work needed on the properties became a team effort. The church's budget afforded expenses for maintenance and repairs, and the property's income provided an extra source of revenue for the church.

As a result of our step of faith, other members responded with similar actions. Deacon Leonard Pena was the first to catch the vision and donated his real property as well. Others followed suit with donations of vehicles and other assets. Net proceeds from the sale of the properties and donations stayed with the church. The payoff from the blessings of giving was enormous. We had gained corporate housing and property rehabilitation experience. Our church was now able to apply for Housing and Urban Development Dept.

(HUD) programs. Proceeds from these programs were now able to employ the faithful volunteers that had labored with us for a worthy cause.

In developing your program ideas and implementing your dreams, you must think "out of the box" and have faith in God.

Think out of the box!

Remember, if you are helping the poor then without a doubt you are doing God's will.

When you are organizing your strategy, remember it is better to do a few things well, than to do a lot of things poorly. Pick an idea or program that you can focus on. You cannot meet all the needs of the community, but you can make a difference in a few people's lives by giving them quality help. Large numbers look good on proposals, but the quality of assistance you provide will be poor. It is better to be realistic than to impress someone.

## Working with Religious Organizations

Earlier we discussed, Can **My Church and Faith Based Organization Work Together? The answer is yes!**

Often churches begin non-profits and pour thousands of dollars into the nonprofit to get it started. The non-profit community organization usually starts out in the church building and utilizes expenses that the church initially bears. When the non-profit begins getting donations and grants the church often wonders if the non-profit can now bear some of the expenses now that it is becoming self-sufficient. The church and the non-profit can work together if certain guidelines can be followed.

First, for the non-profit, any expenses paid from grant funds cannot be used for religious activities. When you apply for a grant you have to submit a budget. The budget must be approved by your grantor. The budget should contain operational expenses that are directly a result of the delivery of services to your target population. An example of these budget line items are rent, staff, utilities, insurance, building maintenance, office supplies, etc.

Churches that house non-profits within their walls can benefit by the nonprofit paying its own expenses. The first thing you must do is make sure the nonprofit is a separate 501 (3) (c) organization. The second important thing is to make sure the non-profit has its own space and that religious worship services are not being held in the same space. This means the non-profit should have its own office or area that it operates in if it is inside a religious building. The next thing you must determine is how much space and time the non-profit uses in the religious facility.

Time is determined by the total time the building is opened for all uses versus the time a non-profit uses the building. Space is determined by measuring the total amount of space in the building versus the total amount of space the nonprofit uses.

When you determine time and space you can set the foundation for how much of the building expenses a non-profit will pay if it is housed in the religious facilities. I will use a realistic scenario to assist you in your calculations.

For example: A building is open for sixty hours per week for church and nonprofit uses. The non-profit uses three offices for case management, administration and counseling. It uses a portion of the fellowship hall for Welfare to Work Classes. The non-profit uses the building for only thirty of the sixty hours it is open. That means the time used is 50 percent. From here you can decide which formula to use when paying utilities. Sometimes your grantor will tell you which one he prefers. He may even ask you to use a combination of both.

The space figures are commonly used to determine rent. In figuring rent use the commercial rent per square foot applicable in your area and multiply the square footage by the allowed commercial rate.

Churches can benefit in supplying the non-profit qualified professionals. If a church member is hired make sure the application and hiring process was fair. The benefit for the church will be a tithe-paying member who contributes to the church and to the community.

Having the non-profit carry its weight can save the church thousands of dollars of repair and expenses. Remember, there is nothing wrong with it, just do it right.

**Does a church have to start a community based or faith based non-profit to deliver services to my community or to get grant money?**

No. There are grants that churches can access. The church must show it has a proven track record of providing a community service aside from religious activities. It must also clearly separate religious funds from funds used for non-religious activities.

There are many churches that have programs such as childcare programs and social services. Each grantor will give the requirements of the organizations that apply. If you are a church please contact the grants administrator for detailed questions about your project.

There are several reasons that a separate non-profit is encouraged, (1) There are more funding options for your faith based non-profit with a separate 501 (3) (c). (2) It will free up your church staff to do ministry. (3) It eases the apprehension of grantors who do not want to be criticized for giving religious organizations money. (4) The accounting and auditing is clean and easier to do.

## A Word of Advice on Politicians

> Date all of them, marry none of them.

You should enter into relationships with your local politician based on a concerted effort to benefit the people of your community. Party politics should not enter the decision making process on delivering your program services. Politics are important when political parties have issues spending money in the program areas you need most. When votes get held up because of party line issues then you need to know who to call to influence their vote and let them know what will happen in your neighborhood if money is not released.

## CHAPTER 6

# Ministry or Program?

While your faith is admirable and your ministry honorable; the grantors are not interested in that side of your organization. Your faith and passion is what drives you to deliver services to your community. Your grantor is interested in your organization's *capacity* to deliver the appropriate services to the citizens of your community.

I'll share this example with you. A Christian minority business owner inquired of proposals that could be written for a coffee shop. She said profits were dwindling and she was barely meeting financial obligations. I inquired of her daily business routines and of her competition in the area. We both came to the conclusion that her Christian theme was not a focal point among avid local coffee drinkers. It was her product variety and location that was key in getting her an edge in the coffee market. Her competitors publicized good ambiance and a wide variety of soft drink products. Her Christian theme provided a place of solace and reflection among customers. A place where those of like faith came together and shared Christian experiences, but she was losing customers because her capacity to deliver a good product was declining.

Have you ever tried to discuss the gospel, let alone have a decent conversation over a bad cup of tea or coffee? It could distract from the social setting and warmth intended to add to the enjoyable discussion of the Word of God.

When it comes to your grantors they are only interested in your ability and capacity to deliver a good service to your clients with the money they give you.

## Implementing Your Community Program

Until an idea is actually put to work it is hard to imagine the logistics of running a program. Wanting to open a food program may involve rewarding work, but do you have the industrial kitchen to cook? Is there a proper place to store food at the right temperatures? Do you have the help to prepare it daily, rain or shine, money or not.

I tell people to visit a program similar to the one you are interested in. Ask the director and staff about the daily operations and challenges it takes to run their program. Ask what keeps them going and what makes them frustrated.

When we began to implement our ideas we went to a conference with many non-profits in attendance. We asked the conference hosts, which organization at the conference was doing housing for homeless persons. We were directed to an agency in a neighboring city that had a similar program. We made an appointment and spent half a day following the director and asking questions. We began our program based on what we learned through our mentor and the unknowns were filled in by experience.

Several years ago our director asked me to start a women's shelter. He gave me three months to have it up and running. We had no training in a women's shelter and I started praying. I told the Lord I needed to speak to a woman who was familiar with the shelter programs, its contracts and agreements. I was sweating because I had no points of reference. Within a week a woman called looking for a transitional housing program. She was a trustee at a shelter. We made an appointment and talked about the logistics of running a shelter. She brought agreements, house rules and everything you could think of to start the shelter. She gave me the do's and don'ts of running a shelter. I was elated that God had answered my prayers. The rest of my questions were answered with experience. The women's shelter is successfully up and running.

# CHAPTER 7

# No Heroics, Please

> The best approach to delivering services to people is a realistic, non-heroic approach.

Now that you have a great program, you have to run it. That means that unless you are running an environmental program or a program to benefit animals, most of the time you have to deliver your services to real live human beings.

With issues involving people in poverty we tend to want to be heroic. We get a savior complex and want to help the world out of their situations. My advice to you is to understand what God said about the poor. In Proverbs 31:9 he said, "Open thy mouth, judge righteously, and plead the cause of the poor and needy." You must ask questions and do your intake process, objectively access the situation and minister judgment or provide the correct service to remedy the problem.

As you progress in your program your savior complex will wear off. The rose colored glasses will break and you may become totally disappointed in humanity.

The best approach to delivering services to people is a realistic, non-heroic approach.

Understand that some of your clients may never come back and say thank you, but you have got to deliver your services based on the set of program criteria that qualifies people to receive your services. Try to assist them with the best you can offer. Experience will teach you how to work with people and still receive fulfillment rather than frustration.

Humans come in all sizes, colors and shapes. They have all kinds of issues, beliefs and value systems. They come in different religions too. Some are sincere and some are dishonest. As God commanded us to help all the poor he never asked us to distinguish between the good, the bad or the ugly. Just help them.

Proverbs 29:7 says that the righteous consider the cause of the poor and the wicked regard not to know it. If you are a just person you will understand the plight or the cause of poverty because you will have taken the time to study and understand the reasoning behind the drama and logistics of poverty. If you have experienced poverty yourself then use your experience to help someone else.

My family personally experienced homelessness and wanted to aid people who experienced the same frustrations. We opened the doors to our non-profit to everyone. We did not know that there were people who were not interested in our help. We did not understand how to help the mentally ill homeless or how to spot a system abuser. As a result we had an 80 percent failure rate for our first year. We learned on our own to set some guidelines for entry into our program and take people who are willing to help themselves if we empowered them. If we did not have the resources to help, then we found someone who could. Our success rate began to rise.

As a result of our willingness to find the resources in our community to help families, we developed a comprehensive list of agencies that could provide help to our clients. Our intake clerks began to get so good at finding help we started getting calls from public service agencies to aid in finding assistance for their clients.

Applying patience to our clients helped us to work through ignorance, defense mechanisms and paranoia. What really makes our jobs worth it is the success stories that we can remember from day to day when the going gets tough. To see the progress your clients make from the pit of hell to owning their own homes and having jobs is worth the trouble you go through on the bad days. You will learn to measure success in the impact you have on one life at a time. If they fail, know that you have done your best job to empower them with the necessary tools to succeed in life.

> **When you pray for a blessing, expect God to say yes!**

One summer our organization was awarded over a half-million dollars for an innovative project. The funds had to be spent in three months. Our plan was to fund eleven community and faith based non-profits who were qualified to do the job. Because of timing issues, we did not have any time to post a request for a proposal.

The dream of a lifetime! We were off to seek grantees for this project. In hand we had an approval letter from our grantor. With the pressure of a grand opening looming over us, we had eleven days to be up and running. The cynicism of our opponents was running rampant and pre-empted our efforts to find grantees. We knocked on doors, visited non-profits and shared our program. The problem was that no one believed us. So we switched to faith-based organizations. We had only a handful of believers there too. We found our eleven organizations. All were faith-based or controlled by people of faith. After our grand opening we received a flood of media attention. Interested parties and late believers flooded our phone lines wanting to be funded after our program was up and running.

One of our grantees taught me an invaluable lesson. When you pray for a blessing, expect God to say yes! We found her organization by way of phone referrals from people we never knew. The initial meeting with the Chief Executive and administrator was at an old fashioned spirit-filled revival. When we had our meeting it was in the church fellowship hall. The CEO was the pastor and the administrator was his sister. We explained that we wanted to fund them because of their location and we believed they could do the program. The administrator broke down crying saying that she had been praying for this to happen and now her blessing had found her.

They did well in the program but at the beginning they hesitated on spending all of the money that was theirs. With a little more training we encouraged her to spend her money. It was hers, she prayed for it! What will you do if God says yes? Are you prepared to win? Are you ready for the rain? It is God who directs time and events. He has not forgotten your prayers, ready or not here He comes!

I like to use the analogy of a fine tuned car. Your grantor is looking for you with all cylinders working. When you begin your organization you may be coughing and sputtering but you are still running. You may backfire once in a while but he knows you're around. He calls you to conferences and meetings and the better you get the smoother you run. Your grantor sees you and when the time is right he will pick your car. All the vehicles he is looking at do different things and they serve a specific purpose to your grantor.

If your grantor is a **PJ** or **Project Jurisdiction** (city, county, town or municipality) he must work with non-profits in the form of a coalition. Your grantor is mandated by the federal government to prove that he is working with the representatives of the community that provides services to families in that community. If your non-profit runs pretty good your grantor will want to comply with federal regulations by giving you some gas (cash) to run community programs.

Your level of experience determines who drives. For new non-profits it is permissible if your grantor drives for a while, but when you can, take the wheel. Your grantor has good intentions, but does not have the passion or the vision for your organization.

> Grantors are looking for good non-profits to deliver services.

Using the analogy of a vehicle, sometimes your PJ will drive a bus and invite you and other experiened non-profits on board. The PJ will take the lead position in a grant and ask you to partner with him and provide services applicable to the grant request. This is the optimum relationship grantors are looking for. Coalitions and partnerships provide for the maximum services delivered to a client.

Don't forget! Once in a while your organization will need a tune up or an overhaul, don't wait until you break down to get serviced. Take a step back and look at all you are doing from time to time and reorganize to provide optimum results to your community.

# CHAPTER 8

# Critics: You Can't Get Rid of Them, but You Don't Have to Listen

When you are doing community faith based work, please remember, only what you do for Christ will last. In the end you will probably be recognized for what you did in this life after you die. Appreciate the flowers and recognition you get for your programs while you are living, but do everything for the glory of God.

If God promised you something concerning what he will do for you in your community then you must stay focused. It is the enemy's job to cause situations and circumstances to keep all attention on the problems you are having instead of God's promise to you. To be successful you must stay focused. Do not turn to the right or the left, but look to Christ and wise counsel for your deliverance.

Countless times I have been to public meetings or conferences. Inevitably, during Q&A someone always stands up and complains about how the establishment is against them or that someone is prejudice against their community efforts. Most of the time everything they are saying is true. In these cases the question to ask yourself is; how much time do you want to dedicate to fighting establishments or accusations? Pick your fights carefully. Determine the cost. If the cost is too high or time consuming quickly move on.

I want to challenge you to understand that if you are faith based and believe that God has you on assignment then you will be attacked. You will intimidate the antiquated establishments in your community, the "not in my back yard" spirit will definitely kick in and people will question your motives.

If you are a mover and shaker expect the enemy to attempt to move and shake you. If you are making a difference in the lives of people expect the enemy not to care about yours.

Stop complaining. What people say about you and your faith-based program should have no regard on the good community work that you will be doing. What they say does not change the fact that there will be someone who needs housing, a meal or clothing. In the time you spend concentrating on a problem, you could have written a grant to pay for a much needed staff member or for funds to help someone pay for their utility costs. Critics will always be with you. You must determine whom you will serve and what you will react to.

The important thing to is to keep focused and listen to the wise and sound advice of people who support you and are working along with you.

# CHAPTER 9

# Checks and Balances

Plan to empower people. The object is to give people a leg up without crippling them. Helping a person too much will backfire every time. It usually causes them to turn on you and blame you for all their problems. Crippling people in this manner makes the muscles of self-will and hope weak and useless. Develop a plan of balances and checks through your staff members so that your strategies are not hindering people from helping themselves.

Those checks and balances include:

1.  Not making hasty decisions. Make your program decisions based on a set of criteria. Some of your clients will need help in emergency situations others can wait for a reasonable amount of time. Planning for this will make it easy on your staff and clients.
2.  Not making decisions without supervisory or staff support.
3.  Review of records by your staff. Occasionally pull some of your own records and make sure your record keeping is accurate.
4.  Discussion of potential problems with board or staff members to come up with viable solutions.
5.  Having a set of rules and guidelines to set entry/exit standards for your community program.
6.  Having a grievance process for your clients.

# CHAPTER 10

# Accountability

Granting agencies want to make sure your office procedures are professional and your staff represents their money well. When you can afford it, get an accountant you can work well with. A good accountant will guide you through I.R.S. reports, non-profit and grant reporting requirements. If your organization is young you can keep your books on Quicken or Quick Books and see an accountant once or twice per year. As you grow you will need an accountant service monthly.

Here is an important note about your intake process. Your intake process needs to start right at the beginning of your program. If you do not have one then you will encounter major problems with the capacity and growth of your organization.

The intake process is the way you will receive a client into your program. This will consist of a volunteer or staff as a point of contact when people come to you for help. For everyone you help you must collect information. Your staff will be assisting people with this process and collecting information on them for the purpose of reporting to your funding source that you actually need the money you are asking for. If you do not have a funding source, keep accurate records. You will use this information to create a monthly report to show how many people you help, what age, race and income range they fall in. As you grow, the information required is much more detailed, but this is good for starters. When you write grants or tell people about the population you serve, you will use the information you collect as a basis for your narrative or speech.

You can make up your own form. It should consist of names of all family members in household, income and source of income for heads of household, current or latest address, phone or message number, age, race and sex of all family members, reason for needing assistance, space for important notes, copy social security numbers of heads of household and current I.D and any other pertinent questions related to the service you offer.

At some point you should look into an automated system. It will not replace the client folder, but it will aid you in keeping your statistics correct. As you help more people it will become difficult to count and track your statistical data manually. You can develop your own or your grantor's may supply their own computerized programs to input your information.

## Non Profit Does Not Mean "No Profit"

A non-profit corporation is run like any corporation. It must have a board, an accounting system, an employer identification number, articles, bylaws, state and federal tax exemptions, office procedures etc. Whether you are big or small you will have some form of all of these in place.

A corporation will have income and expenses. The bottom line is that the revenue left over after the expenses will show that you have made money. The general difference between a non-profit and a for profit is (1) what you call the revenue after expenses and (2) what you do with the revenue you have after expenses. A for profit will pay taxes on the money they have made and can invest or spend the money on any lawful means they deem necessary.

> Non-profits should make profit. The profit is revenue that is left over after expenses.

A non-profit corporation must take their expenses and recycle them back into the non-profit for non-profit use only. Revenue left over after expenses are normally called reserves. Please read your Internal Revenue Guides to determine what laws apply to you and what forms you must file, if any for your non-profit.

Like any business you must exercise good stewardship over what God has blessed you with. When you make or submit a budget you will be telling your board or your grantor where your income is coming from and how you plan to spend it. A budget consists of income sources and expenses. Each item that you list is called an item. That is where the name line items come from. On your budget you may have several line items indicating several sources of income. Each source of income has specific expenses associated with it.

Please note that if you have an expense that is not covered by any of your grants you will need to find an income source to cover that expense. You cannot spend money arbitrarily as expenses come up. Your grantors dictate that you must have a plan. Planning will keep your books orderly. When planning your budget think of all costs possible that are associated with your project and include it in your budget summary. If unexpected expenses do come up associated with a particular grantor, the best thing to do is to call your monitor and get pre-approval to adjust other line items to accommodate the new or unexpected expense.

The importance of having a positive cash flow is that it will increase your capacity. You will be able to go to financial institutions and show a track record of revenue left over after expenses. This will allow you to make loans and financial negotiations to increase your capacity in payroll, purchasing equipment and real property.

# CHAPTER 11

# Accountants and Attorneys

Do not let accountants cause you anxiety. Faith-based organizations have been traditionally wary of accountants. It is a true fact that many times we are so busy ministering to people that we do not have time to take care of this very important area. Often we do not know all the rules and laws concerning how we should govern our bank accounts. In our ignorance we do not know how we should pay ourselves and what expenses should be considered corporate or personal. Welcome to the club! As faith-based organizations, if you don't know you must get some advice.

One of our grantors asked for an audit. So I looked for an auditor that was right for our organization. I explained how our non-profit community programs worked. I also explained how our church worked, our biblical and administrative beliefs and how we handled our funds etc. He was more than happy to help us (for a fee, of course) and point out ways we could do better. He also informed us of any financial and administrative practices that would get us in trouble if we did not change them. It is counter-productive to your accountant's business to discourage you by practicing tactics that would intimidate you into not seeking his professional advice. Remember, you are paying him a fee for his services. Over the years our CPA has kept us out of trouble and given us wise counsel during troubled times.

Before you begin writing proposals, keep statistics. You will need them. You cannot get money without them. You must show the capacity to help people. You must show quantifiable increases in the level of assistance to people to get monies or you must show new program efforts within you organization to get monies. At the end of this book you will find the form you will need to keep your statistics.

# Attorneys

I don't mind being transparent and letting you know that I have needed the advice of corporate attorneys. With the help of sincere attorneys; negotiations were always made to ensure that our corporate interests were always protected. How did we do that? By picking good attorneys that will tell you the truth regardless of whether you like it or not.

Pick an attorney when you are not in trouble or at least pick one that will negotiate in peace before the situation gets out of hand. Remember, you may win your case or disagreement but you will have to live in the community in which your issues arose. Use tact, wisdom and the multitude of counsel.

# Chapter 12

# What am I Signing? Contracts

Every contract you sign will be slightly different. Some will be as simple as a few paragraphs and others will be lengthy legal documents. In every contract you will find the following boilerplate or legal lingo that is the same in almost every contract:

**Read your contracts carefully!**

## The provisions of a contract outline the following:

**Scope of Work**: This outlines what is expected of you and follows closely with what you said you would do, when the contract begins and ends and what your total compensation or award will be. It also talks about compliance with laws and assurances that you will not discriminate. Your contract talks about your budget and what options you will have if there are any changes to it.

**Legal and Insurance requirements**: The contract will spell out what the grantor will expect in the case of a law suit and what type of liability and workman's compensation insurance you are required to have while accepting funds from them.

**Termination clauses:** These are very important. They discuss how your contract will be terminated and under what circumstances. They also go over any reasons that your grantor would hold back any of your payments.

# CHAPTER 13

# What Else Do I Have to Do for My Money?

## Program Monitoring and Reports

> **Monitors and reports are necessary to make sure you meet your goals.**

Monitors are people or agencies hired by your grantor to make sure you are complying with their contracts or program rules. They want to make sure you are doing all that you said in your grant.

Your monitor should also be able to provide technical assistance on problems you may be having in your program.

My Aunt Geraldine gave me the best advice in the world when I first started. She told me that my Uncle Lloyd monitored programs and testing facilities when he worked at Princeton University. Her advice was to run my program like someone was going to walk in at any moment and go through my files and records.

There are different types of program monitoring.

The least involves filling out a report of your program and financial activities monthly and/or annually. Extensive monitoring can come in the form of an onsite financial and/or a program audit. A financial review may take the form of a review of your actual receipts or expense forms or an in depth audit. A program audit will review your client files to see if you are documenting the services you said you would provide. Reviewing your client files will tell your monitor if you are serving the correct service population.

Monitors usually come out to your program site at least two or three times per year and want an overview of your program. They will send you advance notice of their visit and tell you what to expect when they come. When they come they will review your contract as it pertains to what they are supposed to monitor.

They will ask to see your operations, talk with volunteers or employees, look through your program files, check your most recent insurance documents and want to see how you keep your filing system or computer records.

Create a compliance drawer to keep important documents organized.

I suggest keeping a compliance drawer. A compliance drawer is a drawer or two in your filing cabinet solely dedicated to keep your contracts, insurance papers, invoices, related correspondence, deeds, authorizations, articles, bylaws, non-profit exemption papers etc. You may want to keep these things in binders neatly stored in your administrative office. However you keep them, keep it neat and accessible. The last thing you want to do in front of a monitor is look unorganized and unprofessional.

Monitors may want to see how you keep financial records as it pertains to their program and they may want to speak to your CPA. Monitoring visits can take up to two hours or can be several days. If there are deficiencies, your monitor will discuss them with you and write you a letter outlining any problems you may have and the remedy it will take to fix them.

Most monitors will give you time to fix your problems and then check back with you within a reasonable time for proof of compliance.

To lessen the stress on you and your organization, I suggest keeping an open line of communication with your monitor. Dropping a line or an email about your progress or general comments about an upcoming conference will open dialogue with your monitor to assist you with any problems you might be struggling with.

Every grant requires reports. Please turn them in on time. Every grantor gets their money from a larger pot of money to fund you. In order to get their money they must collect data to report to their funding source. This ensures that the flow of money reaches them and they can fund you.

# Chapter 14

# When Do I Get My Money?

Let's Recap:

| **You're almost there!** |
| --- |

A. You had a dream
B. Got Your Team together!
C. Developed Your Dream!
D. You wrote your grant
E. Received an award letter (You got it!)
F. The time between getting your award letter and implementing your program is when your grantor sends you more paperwork to formalize exactly what you said you would do for contract purposes. These amount to technical submissions of your program and ask for information that matches the grant you submitted. At this time the grantor usually calls all the awardees in and trains them on reporting and invoicing.
G. Implemented your program.
H. After you have implemented your program you will be billing your grantor approximately every 30 days for costs you have incurred in your program. Along with the billing you will be sending in reports concerning the progress of your program.

Most arrangements with grantors are by reimbursement only. You must do some planning at this point. You must be able to carry the costs of your program for at least thirty to sixty days until you receive reimbursement for your costs. The wisest thing to do is to make an arrangement with your bank or financial institution for a revolving loan or overdraft agreement equal to at least two months of program costs.

Some grantors will allow a draw for start up costs. Be sure to ask those questions in your training sessions.

## Very Important!!!!

Do not spend any money unless you have signed a contract. Your grantor is not liable for any reimbursements prior to contract signing. If they give you permission to begin a program prior to contract signing, GET IT IN WRITING!

## How Long Does It Take to Get My Money?

Below is an **imaginary timeline** that most grants will follow from the grant writing to the award letter.

| Date | Action | Purpose |
|------|--------|---------|
| October 1 | Request for proposal from the granting agency. | To publicly announce a request for a proposal to all interested parties |
| October 23 and November 5 | Workshops given by the granting agency | To provide agencies with a chance to ask questions and understand the process of the purpose of the grant. This is also training for filling out the grant application. |
| December 15 | Grant Applications are due on this date | The deadline for turning in your completed grant. |
| December 15 to January 15 | Staff reviews your grant to make sure it meets initial criteria. You will receive a letter confirming that they received your grant application. | To make sure your application complies with the application instructions. If it does not meet the initial cut it ends up in the reject pile at this point. |
| January 15 to March 1 | Staff passes your application to a grant reviewer or a citizens committee | You passed the first test. Now people are tearing your grant up and reviewing it. |

| Date | Action | Purpose |
|------|--------|---------|
| March 1-15 | The review committee has scored your grant based on criteria set by the grantor. The reviewers make recommendations. The staff accepts or rejects the recommendations. If your grant comes from a town or city with a council, then a meeting is held and the council meets to hear recommendations. At this point they approve or disapprove publicly. | The committee makes recommendations to the grantor on who they feel should be funded by a scoring system. |
| April 1 | Award letters are sent out. | To congratulate you and inform you of upcoming training for program reporting etc. |
| May 1 | Grantees have 1-2 day training. | To become familiar with reporting requirements ad contracts |
| June 1 | This is the first day of operations or the first day of the program for which you can be reimbursed | |
| July 1-10 | You will submit your first invoice for reimbursement for your program costs for the month of June. | This applies if you are on a reimbursement system * See below for the draw system. |
| August 15-30 | This is the approximate time you will receive reimbursement for June's invoice. | |

**\* Draw system: Your grant may be on the draw system. The draw system will have you access a secure site via telephone in which you can ask for regular draw downs once per month directly into your account. You will be trained to keep your own expenses and draw requests on forms provided by your grantor. At a later date your monitor will ask you for a copy of the expenses to equal your budget requests.**

In the previous table, you can see eight months have passed since you wrote the grant until the day you begin your program. It is for this reason that you must plan in advance for future programs and funding. You want to create several streams of income so your organization will not fold up if you lose one or two sources of income. In the beginning you may be applying for grants that are only a year in length. As the capacity of your non-profit grows it is wise to plan three to five years in advance and look for appropriate funding streams to support you for that amount of time.

# CHAPTER 15

# All Things Work Together

Proverbs 24:3 says, "Through wisdom is an house builded, and by understanding is it established: and by knowledge shall the chambers be filled with all precious and pleasant riches."

As God gives you wisdom you will build your community programs. By understanding the people you help you will establish your program in the community that you serve. With the knowledge you gain you will be able to add different aspects and departments to your program that will be invaluable to your community.

The following points are very important to remember as you begin your journey into faith based community work.

**Pray:** "The effectual, fervent prayer of a righteous man availeth much" (James 5:16b). The prayer of a man who is righteous accomplishes much and brings him power for ministry. In Ephesians 1:17 Apostle Paul tells us to pray "the Father of glory, may give you the spirit of wisdom and revelation in the knowledge of him."

Constant, effectual and fervent prayer will keep you in touch with your spiritual C.E.O, Jesus. Never forget you were called for a purpose in His kingdom and you must communicate with him to keep your mission statement in tune with his.

**Plan:** In Nehemiah, chapter two, Nehemiah does some planning and meditation for a three day meeting in Jerusalem. In verse 12 he has a night meeting with a *few* men. No doubt he surrounded himself with men of faith and purpose. Nay Sayers and doubters were not invited. They arrive to inspect a scene of despair and desolation in the waste of what used to be the home of their fathers.

Because Nehemiah has been in fervent prayer and constant communication with God, he has been given a plan to build by the Master architect, God. He has a strategic planning meeting. He does not tell anyone about the plans God has given him, but uses wisdom in breaking his plan to his executive board.

After he took his executive board on a tour he gathers them and reviews the challenges and issues that are before them. He rallies them with a passionate speech on neighborhood pride and tells them of the hand of God that is upon him and the favor that he has received from the king (president, governor, mayor, councilman) to rebuild the walls of Jerusalem. He shares the personal words of encouragement and support that the king has given him. He then gives the cry for action! "Let us rise and build."

After this rally cry his board and advisors caught the vision and answered with the response "Let us arise and build." The Bible then tells us that they "strengthened their hands for this good work".

**Execute:** Execute means to put an instruction or plan into effect. You must execute the vision that God has given you. Put some legs on it and breathe life into it. Feed it and stroke it. The execution of your plan is the delivery or birth of your dream.

In the Book of First Kings, Solomon partnered with King Hiram of Tyre and executed the dream God placed in him to build the Temple. There were specific instructions for building materials and the measurements of the Temple and laws that governed the labor force. Solomon went about executing the plan and doing everything that God had told him to do in order to get the job done.

An important postscript to the story is that after the Temple was built God spoke with Solomon in 1 Kings 6:11-13 concerning the house which he had built. God never mentioned the physical temple while he talked to Solomon, but was more interested in his spiritual temple. God told Solomon to walk in His statues, *execute* His judgment and keep His commandments.

This is a reminder to put first things first and never forget that God is more interested in a relationship with us than what we do. It is from our good relationship with Christ that we will be able to do our best.

**Evaluate:** The fourth and last point I want to share with you is to evaluate. When you evaluate you will assess the situation. You look at its strong points and its weaknesses and you come to conclusions about whether you have executed your plan in the most effective manner. While we never have to evaluate anything that God puts together, often we must evaluate our own acts because we make mistakes and these mistakes cause delays, interruptions and misunderstandings.

Prior to evaluating the success or failure of your project or program, examine yourself and your relationship with God. Here you will find the secrets of your success or failure. Remember Psalms 37:3-8. Trust in the Lord. Delight in Him and He shall give you the desires of your heart. Commit your ways unto him and he will bring your dreams and prayers to pass. Rest in God and wait patiently for him. Do not be anxious for those who move faster and prosper before you. Cease from anger and forsake wrath, God will take care of all of your affairs.

We wish you the best in all of your endeavors and much success to all of your ventures. We believe the information from this book will be a blessing to you and your organization and hope you share it with others as a testimonial and encouragement.

# EMPOWERING YOU TO HELP ADDENDUM (A)
## Client Assistance Form

Date _____

Name and Title of
interviewer _____

Signature of
interviewer _____

Name(s): _____    Male/Female

Address (as of ) _____

Phone No. _____ Message Phone _____

Birthdate :_____ Social Security # _____

No. of Children _____ Children Ages _____

Children's Sex _____

Are you Disabled? _____ Veteran or Service connected? _____

Income Source _____

How Much _____ Food Stamps$ _____

If you are homeless, how long have you been homeless? _____

Circumstance of homelessness/or problem _____

_____

What does client need? _____

What is your social support (family friends etc.)
Address or phone of support person? _____

_____

What did we do for client? (Direct Service Offered) _____

_____

_____

Job Experience _____

Are you looking work? _____

Where have you applied? _____

_____

Referred by: _____

# About the Author

**Ms. Jenai Morehead** is the Chief Executive Officer of the Jenai Annabelle Morehead Foundation. She is a nonprofit consultant, grant writer, teacher and author. Ms. Morehead provides technical assistance and reviews grants for many faith-based organizations as well as overseas the funding activities of the foundation.

Ms. Morehead lives in Southern California and enjoys the company of her children and grandchildren.

To contact Ms. Morehead for consulting or speaking engagements please email **Jenaimorehead@aol.com**
or visit **Thefoundationconsultants.org**

It is with great pleasure that I share the wonderful things that God has done for me through the knowledge that he has blessed me with. I gladly share it with you so that your non-profit and faith based business ventures go smoothly.

The creation of this book is but a small sum of many years of experience, and the encouragement of many people. I want to thank my family and friends for their patience and love during the time it took to write this book and to my clients who worked through my crude earlier versions.

LaVergne, TN USA
16 April 2010
179550LV00003B/52/P